JUL 2 0 2006

WITHDRAWN

D1505919

Inventions That Shaped the World

THE STEAM ENGINE

TAMRA ORR

Franklin Watts
A Division of Scholastic Inc.
New York · Toronto · London · Auckland · Sydney
Mexico City · New Delhi · Hong Kong
Danbury, Connecticut

JUL 2 0 2006

Photographs © 2005: akg-Images, London: 17, 19; Art Resource, NY: 39 (Giraudon/Conservatoire National des Arts et Metiers, Paris, France), 35 (Archives de l'Ecole Nationale des Ponts et Chaussees, Paris/Archives Charmet), 41 (Private Collection); Brown Brothers: 22; Corbis Images: 5 bottom, 12, 20, 23, 27, 55, 66, 69 (Bettmann), cover top left, chapter openers (Philip Gendreau/Bettmann), 60 (Hulton-Deutsch Collection), cover bottom left (Steve Kaufman), 64 (Minnesota Historical Society), 8 (Michael Nicholson), 14 (Reuters), 25 (Royalty-Free), timeline (Paul A. Souders), 7; Getty Images/Hulton Archive: 26 (Archive Photos), 31 (Haywood Magee), 52 (MPI), 57 (Rischgitz), cover bottom right, 36 (Stock Montage), chapter openers, 10, 46, 48, 53; Mary Evans Picture Library: 21; North Wind Picture Archives: 6, 13, 15, 24, 45, 50; Robertstock.com/P. Degginger: 37; Stock Montage, Inc.: 29, 54; Superstock, Inc./Henry Alexander Ogden: 56; The Art Archive/Picture Desk: 28; The Image Works: 59 (NRM/SSPL), 58 (HIP/Science Museum, London), 32, 33, 61 (SSPL), 18 (Charles Walker/Topfoto).

Illustrations by J. T. Morrow

Cover design by The Design Lab
Book production by The Design Lab

Library of Congress Cataloging-in-Publication Data
Orr, Tamra.
    The steam engine / Tamra B. Orr.
        p. cm. — (Inventions that shaped the world)
    Includes bibliographical references and index.
    ISBN 0-531-12400-2 (lib. bdg.)   0-531-16724-0 (pbk.)
1. Steam-engines—Juvenile literature. I. Title. II. Series.
TJ467.O77 2005
621.1—dc22   2005000777

© 2005 by Tamra Orr.
All rights reserved. Published simultaneously in Canada.
Printed in the United States of America.
1 2 3 4 5 6 7 8 9 10 R 14 13 12 11 10 09 08 07 06 05

Contents

CHAPTER ONE

Entering the Industrial Age

Throughout history, curious men and women have experimented in an attempt to understand their world. After gaining some understanding of how things work, they turned their efforts toward changing the world with their creative inventions. The Wright brothers found a way for humans to fly; Alexander Graham Bell created a way for them to talk when separated by hundreds of miles. Guglielmo Marconi's work with radio

Alexander Graham Bell places the first call on the New York to Chicago telephone line.

Before the steam engine was invented, water wheels often provided the power for mills.

waves eventually allowed people to listen to radios in their homes, while Marie Curie discovered the mysterious element radium, which led to the development of X rays. All of these inventions have made life easier.

The steam engine ushered in a completely new age in history. Until it was invented, power came from wind, water, and animals. All of these sources had disadvantages and were not reliable. Wind could die down; rivers could dry up or freeze over; animals tired and had to rest. Because the steam engine was a dependable source of power, some experts consider it to be the invention that introduced a new era of history called the Industrial Age.

John Lienhard from the University of Houston's College of English says, "Steam engines were England's unique

Great Britain's position as the leader of the Industrial Revolution was celebrated in showcases such as the Great Industrial Exhibition of 1851 in London, England.

gift to the Industrial Revolution. . . . Steam didn't change the English countryside overnight, but it was a stalking horse of revolution. Steam engines were agents of changes that far outreached anything their makers had ever thought of. . . . Steam finally became the highly visible center of the technologies that utterly changed our life on planet Earth." The steam engine lifted a burden from people and beast.

As the seventeenth century came to an end, inventions were changing daily life, especially in England. In 1774, George Louis Lesage *patented* the first electric telegraph.

Looms powered by steam engines revolutionized the manufacture of cloth, making the industry much more efficient.

Cloth manufacturing, an industry that employed many people, was becoming more efficient, thanks to the invention of power looms and the flying shuttle, which allowed workers to weave faster. A self-winding clock, created in 1783, made it easier to keep time, and Benjamin Franklin's invention of bifocal eyeglasses made it easier for some people to see clearly. The creation of the steam engine was part of this age of change.

The steam engine was developed over more than a century. It was finally made practical by combining several individuals' exceptional insights with the knowledge of others who had already explored the same territory. While some inventors in history have frequently kept new ideas secret to prevent others from stealing and claiming the technology, this was not true with the steam engine. Almost every step of its development was published and shared with others.

The Industrial Age began in England in 1769. It was a time in which the demand for power was far greater than the supply. The simple windmills and waterwheels that once provided the energy needed to manufacture goods were no longer enough. Neither were the strong horses and sturdy wheels that had transported everything from water to cargo. It was in this era that machinery started to become complex, and the entire concept of manufacturing changed. Easier transportation became essential to

FOWLER'S PATENT ENGINE AND WINDLASS FOR STEAM-PLOUGHING. *1869.*

Steam plows were one way that the steam engine made farming easier.

success, and the person who could find a way to move things faster was welcomed and respected.

In the case of the steam engine, that honor belonged to three men—Thomas Savery, Thomas Newcomen, and James Watt. By building on each other's ideas, they eventually built a machine capable of doing everything they had hoped for—and far more.

Water, Water, Everywhere

England had a serious problem. It needed a dependable source of power to run textile machines and supply the iron industry. Like the rest of Europe, however, England had almost used up the wood in its forests. Without giving much thought to the fact that the supply might one day run out, people in England had thrown wood into fireplaces to keep homes warm, to cook food, and to maintain farms. Now, with the supply of trees steadily decreasing, the English were becoming more and more dependent on coal for their energy needs.

Coal was plentiful in Great Britain; in fact, it had the largest supply in Europe. The country was also rich in copper and tin. The demand for coal, as well as for other minerals, kept growing. In the 1550s, England was pro-

Coal miners work in a mine in Newcastle, England.

ducing 200,000 tons (181,400 metric tons) of coal. By 1700, that number had risen to 3 million tons (2.7 t) per year. Most of Europe also depended on British coal for their energy needs.

To keep up with the demand, miners kept digging farther underground. Some wealthy landowners even encouraged mining companies to explore their estates in hopes of finding coal. It was not long before this extensive mining caused a problem. Water was leaking into the mines too quickly to control.

Flooding made it challenging to move around in the mine and nearly impossible to find the coal. It was difficult and dangerous work for the miners. Progress would halt while they struggled to remove the water. Some miners depended on simple buckets tied to ropes to haul up the unwanted water. Others used horses to take it away or windmills to pump it out. All of these methods were terribly slow and usually ineffective. Money was lost every time production was halted to drain away the endless water.

Some early steam engines were used to draw coal out of mines. They also were used to help remove water from underground mines when they started to flood.

The delays were embarrassing for England. Miners were motivated to search for something—anything—that would solve this ongoing dilemma. Many people tried to find a solution. Between 1561 and 1642, there were 182 patents filed. One in seven was for some kind of contraption that would keep water out of the mines.

The shortage of fuel eventually became a problem in other parts of the world. By the mid-1800s, the United

Flooding can still be a danger to those who work in coal mines. Water is pumped out of a mine in Quecreek, Pennsylvania, in 2002.

Miners dig coal in Pennsylvania in the 1860s. By the mid-1800s, the United States had begun mining for coal.

States had also used up much of its wood and was starting to dig for coal. Like the British, they soon had flooding problems in their mines and had to shut them down. In time, they began importing steam engines from Great Britain, along with skilled teams to build and operate them.

Early Ideas

In 1630, David Ramsay was granted a patent for a machine that would lift water from the mines. He planned to invent a machine that would do everything from "raise water from lowe pitts by fire" and "make any sort of mills to goe on standing waters by continual moc'on without the help of windes, waite of horse" to "make boates, shippes and barges to goe against the wind and tyde." Despite the patent, there is no evidence that any of Ramsay's ideas went beyond words on paper. Another man who filed a patent and attempted to find ways to remove the water from mines was Edward Somerset, second marquis of Worcester. In the 1660s, he wrote many papers about how such an invention should be built, but he never tested his theories by building one.

The power that came from horses, wind, or waterwheels was not enough to help solve the flooding problem in the mines. Horses were expensive to feed and shelter, and eventually they got too old to work. Windmills worked well—as long as the wind kept blowing. Waterwheels were more dependable, but floods or droughts could shut them down. Emptying the water from the mines was a priority. Coal was absolutely essential for producing the energy to drive machines, provide heat, and keep the world moving forward. In the end, it would take the dedication and ingenuity of several people to find the answer to this ongoing problem.

The Men Behind the Power

Three men deserve the main credit for perfecting the early steam engine. Each one contributed new designs that helped to create the machine. The very first model, however, was created in about A.D. 62, and it was made to be little more than a toy.

In 1654, a German named Otto von Guericke invented a machine he called an air pump. It had the basic elements of a piston (a solid disc that fits

Otto von Guericke was born on November 20, 1602, in Magdeburg, Germany.

An Intriguing Toy

A gifted mathematician named Hero of Alexandria put together the first steam engine. He was known throughout the Roman Empire for his writings about *hydraulics, pneumatics,* and mechanics. He built a working steam engine on a small scale called an *aeolipile,* or "wind ball." He placed a sealed cauldron of water over a fire. As the water began to boil, steam rose into two curved outlet tubes and a hollow sphere. When the steam escaped *tangentially* from two small tubes on the ball, the reaction made the ball spin. In Hero's opinion, this toy was meant for nothing other than entertainment.

Using the same information about the power and ability of steam, Hero also designed self-opening doors for temples. He lit a fire that warmed the air around altars. As the air was heated, it expanded and increased the pressure in a pot of water. The water was forced through a tube into a hanging bucket. The weight of the water made the bucket go down, pulling ropes that were attached to it and to the door. The ropes pulled the doors open. Once the fire was put out, the air pressure decreased, the water returned to the pot, and a counterweight shut the doors.

snuggly into a larger *cylinder,* essentially a plunger pump) in it. He conducted an experiment with his pump in a town called Magdeburg. Many people came to watch. He joined two metal bowl-shaped hemispheres and sealed them together. He pumped out the air from inside the sphere, drawing each side against the other with *atmospheric pressure.* The bond was so tight that not even sixteen horses, eight on each side, could pull them apart. This was the first public demonstration of the force of air!

In 1679, a French physicist and inventor named Denis Papin created a type of piston engine. It was a rather crude machine that he

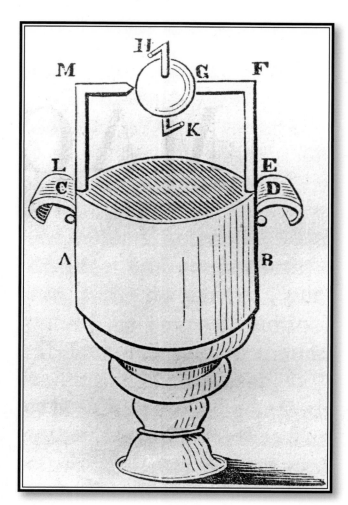

The first steam engine was a toy created by Hero of Alexandria.

19

named the "digester." It is the model for today's pressure cooker, a pot that uses steam under pressure and at a high temperature to cook food quickly. The machine helped to show the relationship between *air pressure* and the temperature at which water boils.

Otto von Guericke demonstrates his air pump.

A Big First Step

The first person to put together what would one day be known as the steam engine was Thomas James Savery. He was born to a well-known family in Shilston, England, in about 1650. Although educated as a military engineer, he spent most of his time inventing and experimenting. He constructed one of the first clocks and designed an arrangement of paddle wheels for ships that could make them move faster and more efficiently. When he tried to market his concept to the British Admiralty, however, he was dismissed rudely for not belonging to the elite organization. Savery installed his invention on some smaller vessels instead. Later in life, he would also invent an *odometer* for ships to measure the distance they traveled over water.

Thomas Savery was a British engineer and inventor who created the first steam engine.

Savery was aware of the flooding problem English miners were facing, and he wanted to find a solution. He created a machine that had no moving parts or valves and had

Savery patented the design for his steam engine in 1698.

to be operated by hand. It worked by heating water until it turned into steam and then putting that steam into a tank. The tank condensed the steam, creating a *vacuum.* This drew water up from the mines. He patented his design in 1698, and the patent stated that it would "be of great use for draining mines, serving towns with water, and for the working of all sorts of mills, when they have not had the

benefit of water nor constant winds." Savery gave a model of his invention to the Royal Society of London. In 1698, he made further improvements to it and presented a model to King William III and his court at Hampton. He called his creation a fire engine. It would later be labeled a steam pump.

William III was the king of England from 1689 to 1702.

In 1698, Savery was awarded a patent for his invention that gave him a fourteen-year monopoly over the steam engine concept. In other words, no one but Savery was allowed to work on a similar project for that time period. The inventor even managed to convince Parliament to extend his patent to 1733, which gave him

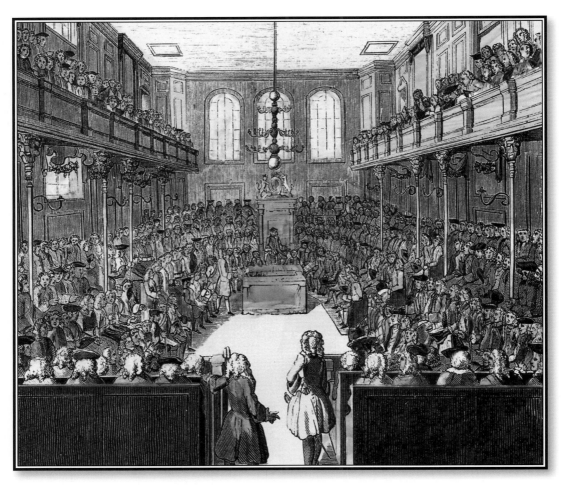

Members of Parliament (shown here) extended Savery's patent to 1733.

an additional twenty-one years. He angered many people by demanding a fee from engineers who used any of his ideas in creating a steam engine.

Savery's fire engine required burning a huge amount of coal to pump out a small amount of water, and it carried the risk of scalding people. This made the invention quite inefficient, as well as potentially dangerous. Despite these problems, Savery widely demonstrated and marketed his fire engine. In 1702, he published a pamphlet describing his invention. The pamphlet was distributed to owners and managers of coal mines. In addition to explaining how the fire engine would help remove water from mines, Savery's pamphlet claimed his invention had the potential to distribute water to palaces and country homes, as well as cities and

Huge amounts of coal were needed to create enough power to pump even a small amount of water out of a flooded mine.

towns. He said the fire engine would deliver a continuous water supply to people in their homes to use for drinking and cooking. Cities and towns would also benefit because they would have a dependable source of water in case of fire.

It's been said that while creating his engine, Savery read a book by Edward Somerset, another inventor who was pursuing the same invention. According to this story, Savery bought all the copies of Somerset's book that he could find and burned them to ensure that only he would get credit for the invention. While most historians do not believe this story, there is a striking resemblance between Savery's and Somerset's illustrations.

Edward Somerset was born in 1601 and died in 1667.

The Blacksmith

Thomas Newcomen was the next man to turn his efforts to the creation of a steam engine. Born in 1663 in Dartmouth, England, Newcomen was a blacksmith, a job that was thought of as low-class.

Because of this, most of his ideas were ignored. After all, many people reasoned, how could a simple tradesperson find the solution to a problem that had baffled some of the most scientific minds? Some people thought of him as more of a schemer than an inventor. Some historians believe that Savery and Newcomen

Replacing the shoes on horses was one of the many common jobs done by a blacksmith.

Newcomen's engine for pumping water out of a mine worked better than Savery's model but was still inefficient.

worked together, and it is certainly possible because they lived only about 15 miles (24 kilometers) apart.

It was Newcomen's background in practical repair and mechanics that allowed him to envision ways to improve Savery's steam pump. In his design, he used atmospheric pressure, or the actual weight of air, to make his model work. His atmospheric steam engine used moving parts, including a piston and a rocking beam. In 1705, Newcomen hired an assistant named John Calley and together they got a patent on their machine. In 1712, they used one of the modified machines to pump water out of a mine. While it worked better than Savery's model did, the piston moved very slowly, and the pump was still inefficient.

Thomas Newcomen died in London in 1729, at the age of sixty-six. Though he was just a simple blacksmith, his is still one of the most honored names in science.

Efficiency at Last

The inventor known as the father of the steam engine was James Watt. Born in the Scottish city of Greenock in 1736, Watt was not a healthy boy and spent much of his childhood at home, rather than school. He was taught at home by his parents and spent most of his time reading, sketching, carving, and making models out of metal and wood. As a

James Watt was born in 1736 and died in 1819.

child, he constructed a working *barrel organ* and often repaired neighbors' broken instruments. At age eleven, he returned to school and endured much teasing and tormenting from students who did not understand the frail, serious young man.

Teakettle Science

Legend has it that James Watt was fascinated by mathematical equations from a very young age. Some biographies state that Watt was doing geometry at six years old and that watching how steam was created by heating water in his mother's teakettle inspired his first interest in the power of steam.

In 1750, Watt's aunt watched her nephew's fascination with a teakettle. She thought his behavior was quite odd. "James, I never saw such an idle boy!" she said. "Take a book or employ yourself usefully. For the last half hour you have not spoken a word, but taken off the lid of that kettle and put it on again, holding now a cup and now a silver spoon over the steam; watching how it rises from the spout, and catching and counting the drops of hot water it falls into."

When Watt was eighteen, he went to Glasgow, where he worked as a mathematical instrument maker. He spent a year making parts of *quadrants* and *compasses* for ships' navigators. Poor health forced him to move back home, but the following year he headed off to London to see if he could get another job creating these

The University of Glasgow was founded in 1451 and is the second-oldest university in Scotland.

instruments. He could not find one; the trade unions would only hire those with formal training, and he didn't have any. Finally, in 1757, a friend at the University of Glasgow hired Watt to repair classroom instruments such as compasses and telescopes. One of his tasks at the university changed his life.

A Newcomen steam engine that was used in classroom demonstrations had broken, and Watt was given the task of repairing it. He had little trouble doing so, but found himself inspired to see if he could make some improvements to the design. What he came up with eventually became the dominant design for the working steam engine. It was far more efficient, thanks to the new concept of separating the condenser and cylinder. Watt received a patent for his invention in 1769.

In 1774, Watt partnered with Matthew Boulton, an industrialist from Birmingham. It was Boulton's factory

Watt's separate condenser model greatly improved the efficiency of the steam engine.

Watt and Boulton established their Soho steam engine factory near Birmingham, England.

that produced and sold the steam engine Watt created. His company became one of the most successful manufacturing plants in the world. It housed workshops, showrooms, offices, and stores for a variety of trades and was known for producing high-quality jewelry, silverware, and plated goods. Boulton was not an inventor like Watt, but he was an excellent businessman, a perfectionist, and a problem solver. The two men applied for and received an extension on the patent for Watt's steam engine that lasted until 1800.

An Epiphany

One Sunday, because Scottish law forbade people to work on the Sabbath, Watt decided to take a stroll. Watt headed for a meadow along a riverbank. It was there that he finally figured out an essential element for his steam engine.

"I had entered the Green by the gate at the foot of Charlotte Street, and had passed the old washing house. I was thinking upon the engine at the time, and had gone as far as the herd's house, when the idea came into my mind that, as steam was an elastic body, it would rush into a vacuum, and, if a communication were made between the cylinder and an exhausted vessel, it would rush into it, and might be there condensed without cooling the cylinder. I then saw that I must get rid of the condensed steam and injection water if I used a jet, as in Newcomen's engine. Two ways of doing this occurred to me: First, the water might be run off by a descending pipe, if an offjet could be got at the depth of 35 or 36 feet [10 or 11 meters], and any air might be extracted by a small pump. The second was, to make the pump large enough to extract both water and air. I had not walked farther than the Golf house, when the whole thing was arranged in my mind."

Between 1781 and 1785, Watt obtained patents for the *double-acting engine,* the *smokeless furnace,* and *parallel motion.* The double-action engine allowed the piston to exert power in two directions, instead of just one. The

Watt continued to improve on his steam engine, altering the design to make the engine move faster and take up less space.

smokeless furnace enabled mills to use steam to run their machinery. Parallel motion made his engine move faster and take up less room. Years later, Watt told his son, "Though I am not over anxious after fame, yet I am more proud of the parallel motion than of any other mechanical invention I have ever made."

Watt died in 1819, at the age of eighty-four. He was buried at Saint Mary's Handsworth, Birmingham, near his friend and partner Boulton. Today, he is remembered whenever a unit of power called a watt is used (746 watts equal 1 horsepower); it was named after him to honor his contribution to science and invention.

Not a Lone Genius

"Watt has suffered a fate similar to that of Thomas Alva Edison, whose name perhaps more than any other has come to symbolize inventive 'genius,' associated as it is with the phonograph, electric light bulb and even moving pictures. Yet neither worked in a vacuum. Where Edison, in his 'invention factory,' was surrounded by support staff, Watt, too, had always relied on others. Family, connections, partners, friends, craftsmen, factory workers, agents, patrons, politicians, propagandists, lawyers and philosophers crowded Watt. This was the society of steam that made his achievements possible. Hard as they tried to embellish the image, Watt was no more a lone genius than Edison."

—Ben Marsden, 2002

From Pump to Engine

Today, the steam engine seems like such an obvious machine that it can be hard to understand why it took so many brilliant minds so many years to make it a practical, efficient piece of equipment. It is important to realize that before a steam engine could even be imagined, several basic concepts had to be understood. Inventors had to be able to recognize the idea of a vacu-

Today, steam-powered trains are not considered advanced technology. When the steam engine was first created, however, it was thought of as an amazing, cutting-edge invention.

um and how to create one. They also had to understand how air pressure worked, how to generate steam, and what a cylinder and a piston were. All of this knowledge took time to develop, and some of these concepts would not be completely understood for decades.

A Word from Author Robert Thurston

In *A History of the Growth of the Steam Engine,* Robert Thurston wrote, "The wonderful progress of the present century is, in a very great degree, due to the invention and improvement of the steam engine, and to the ingenious application of its power to kinds of work that formerly taxed the physical energies of the human race."

A First Attempt

Simply stated, a steam engine is a device that converts pressure to mechanical force. The first practical design for such a machine came from Thomas James Savery, and it was more of a pump than an engine. It had no moving parts, and its valves had to be turned by hand. Savery knew that when water boils, it turns to steam and expands to approximately 1,700 times its liquid volume. He also knew that when steam is suddenly cooled, it creates a vacuum that can be filled with a gas or liquid. Savery used these ideas to create a pump that could help miners with their flooding problem. The valves he used in his model were turned to let steam enter a sealed vessel. Then cold water was poured onto the vessel to chill it and condense the steam. This created a vacuum, which sucked water from the mine into a pipe.

Savery's pump worked, but it was very slow and inefficient. It required a great deal of coal to pump only a small amount of water. It was clear that while Savery

Savery's pump worked but still posed several problems.

was on the right track, improvements were needed to make his invention a success.

A Second Try

Thomas Newcomen knew of Savery's fire engine and suspected that he could make changes to it that would improve it immensely. The major change Savery made in the design was in using the natural force of atmospheric pressure, or the pressure exerted by the earth's atmosphere, to do the hard work of pumping water. His model came to be known as the atmospheric engine.

Newcomen added a domed boiler, a vertical cylinder, and a piston. His model sent steam into a cylinder, and the steam was condensed by cold water that was sprayed onto the cylinder. This created a vacuum within the cylinder, and then atmospheric pressure was used to push a piston in downward strokes. The piston, which hung from one end of a large horizontal beam, was then pulled back up by heavy pump rods at the other end of the beam, where pressure would push it down again. Each stroke of the piston would bring about 10 gallons (38 liters) of water to the surface.

The Newcomen engine was much bigger than previous models, reaching two stories high. The cylinders were up to 6 feet (1.8 m) in diameter. They were originally made of brass, but when brass became too expensive the cylinders were made out of iron instead. Newcomen's model was a definite improvement because the intensity of the pressure was not limited by the pressure of steam, but by atmospheric pressure. Although this model was more powerful and reliable than Savery's, it was still slow and used a great deal of fuel. In addition, the rapid heating and cooling caused wear in the metal cylinder. James Watt's ingenuity was still needed to turn the steam engine into a real success.

The Third Time Around

Although both Savery and Newcomen's models were quite innovative, they used too much fuel to be efficient. When Watt got the opportunity to repair a broken Newcomen engine while he was

Newcomen's "Engine to Raise Water by Fire" was a much more powerful model than Savery's.

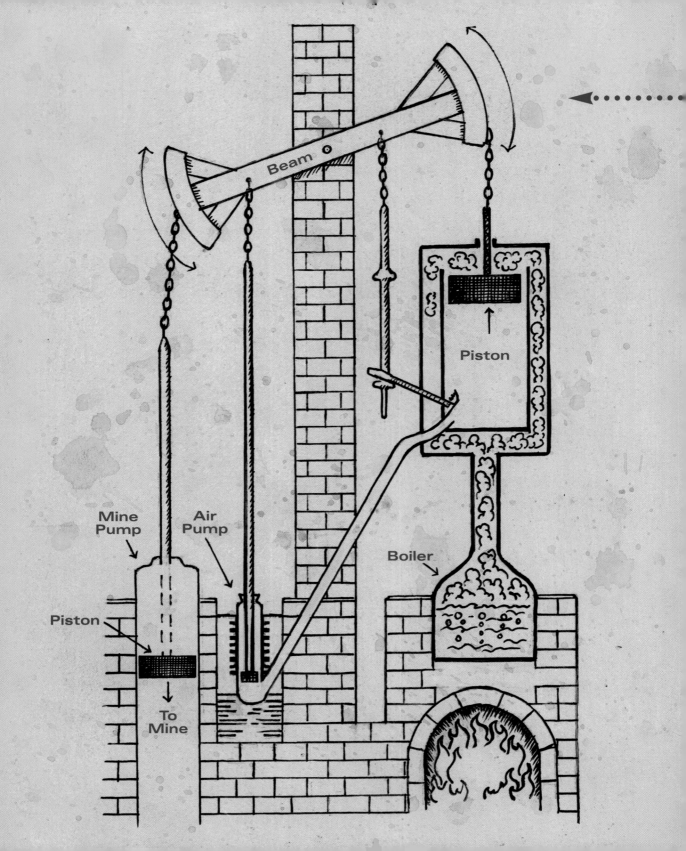

How Does It Work?

To create an effective steam engine, you must first have an enclosed boiler in which to heat water. In this early Watt steam pump from 1776, the water is heated to boiling by a coal or wood fire. At this point, the water turns to steam and expands 1,700 times in volume. The steam passes out of the boiler through a pipe, past two valves, and goes into the closed end of the cylinder. Inside the cylinder is a snug-fitting round disk called a piston. It has a rod attached to it and can slide up and down within the cylinder. When the steam enters the cylinder under pressure, it pushes against the piston and moves it. The repetition of this movement is what makes the engine work.

working at the University of Glasgow, he glimpsed his chance to improve it. He realized the main problem with his colleague's model was that the cylinder had to be heated up and then cooled immediately over and over again. Not only was this hard on the metal, but the pump could not keep up with the heating and reheating the design required. It was obvious why it took so much fuel to operate. How could Watt get around this problem?

After much thought, Watt came up with the solution. He designed a steam engine that used two separate cylinders. In this model, one cylinder would be used for cooling and the other for expansion. They were connected through a valve. The condenser produced the vacuum needed and kept the insulated cylinder hot at the same time.

Watt's colleague, Professor Joseph Black, recalled the moment Watt worked it all out. "The fortunate thought

No Great Effort

Reflecting on his engine, Watt once said to Professor George Jardine, "When analyzed, the invention would not appear so great as it seemed to be. In the state in which I found the steam engine, it was no great effort of mind to observe that the quantity of fuel necessary to make it work would forever prevent its extensive utility. The next step in my progress was equally easy to inquire what was the cause of the great consumption of fuel. This, too, was readily suggested, viz., the waste of fuel which was necessary to bring the whole cylinder, piston, and adjacent parts from the coldness of water to the heat of steam, no fewer than from 15 to 20 times in a minute."

occurred to him of condensing the steam by cold in a separate vessel or apparatus, between which and the cylinder a communication was to be opened for that purpose every time the steam was to be condensed; while the cylinder itself might be preserved perpetually hot. . . . This capital improvement flashed on his mind at once, and filled him with rapture." Watt's early engines leaked steam because at the time, there was no tool capable of machining a perfectly round hole. Steam would leak out around the piston. In 1775, the British inventor John Wilkinson developed a *boring machine* that could produce better cylinders. In the following years, the planer was also invented, which improved the steam engine by smoothing out the surfaces of its different parts.

Watt's model used steam pressure rather than atmospheric pressure. Along with the separate cylinders, Watt's later design also used a piston that would give power in both directions, instead of just one as in Newcomen's

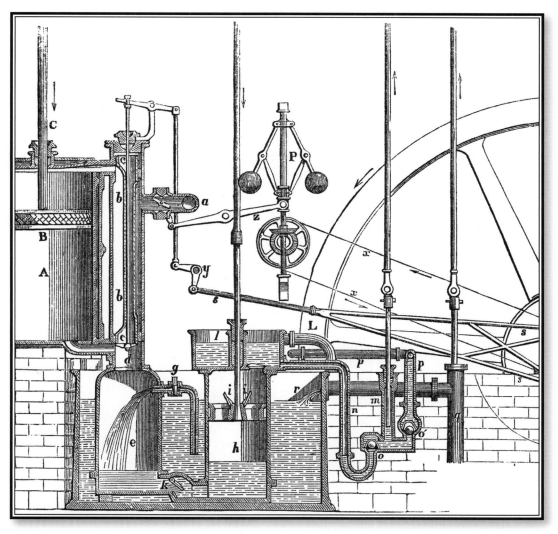

Watt's steam engine with two separate cylinders was a big improvement in the machine's efficiency.

A worker operates a boring machine in the late 1800s. A boring machine drills holes in metal.

model. Later, that was replaced with a system of gears, and then by a crankshaft. Although they did not know it, Watt and his partner, Matthew Boulton, had created the heart of the first locomotive and steamboat. Watt also created a double-action system that allowed steam into each end of the engine's cylinder and throttle valves that controlled the amount of steam allowed into the chamber and the speed of operation.

It was not long before Boulton suggested to Watt that the steam engine had the potential to help more than just miners. He thought the machine could be used in mills as well. "I think that mills present a field that is boundless and that will be more permanent than these transient mines," he stated, "and more satisfactory than these inveterate, ungenerous and envious miners and mine lords." In response, Watt invented a different type of steam engine called a rotative steam engine that could be used for driving machinery in factories.

Although this new model proved to be much more efficient and used three-quarters less fuel, Watt was frightened to use it, especially in the mines. Because of the heat and pressure required to run it, there had been accidents in which people had died. Watt was afraid that one of his engine's boilers would explode and kill a great many workers. He was so adamant that high-pressure steam not be used that he refused to do any experiments based on the

The rotative steam engine could be used to drive machinery in mills and factories.

concept. He even suppressed the working model one of his assistants created so that the process would not be discovered. Watt's refusal to use this new steam engine upset some people, but inspired others. As Watt's patent approached its expiration date, many British and U.S. scientists were more than eager to take over and find out how high-pressure steam might change the world.

The Engine Expands

The steam engine opened the door to a new era in history. It made possible many of the inventions that were a part of the Industrial Revolution. It helped change the world from an agricultural society based on farming and crops to an industrial one based on factories and mass production. It affected everything from the way families scheduled their days to how new lands were discovered. Steam power brought a reliable, strong source of power to people for the first time in history.

Before the steam engine, the economy in Europe and the United States was based on agriculture. Families rarely left their hometown; it was where they lived, worked, and died. In many ways, people were slaves to nature, depending on the unpredictable temperature,

Before the steam engine was invented, most people in Europe and the United States made their living by farming.

rainfall, and angle of the sun to grow their crops and produce an income. The steam engine changed all that. Suddenly, factories were being built everywhere. Before the steam engine, they had to be located near a source of water or wind to generate power, but now they could be built anywhere. As factories grew, more jobs were created. People left their farms and villages to work away from the home. Time became far more important as employees were expected to arrive at work at a certain time and put in a specific number of hours. Steam-driven implements that could plow the ground at least twenty times faster than before helped those families that did remain on the farm.

Other people capitalized on the work of Watt and his predecessors and created the steamboat and the steam locomotive. These two inventions changed the face of transportation, making the movement of people and goods faster and easier. This opened up trade where it wasn't possible before. Cities grew as their populations increased because people found it much easier to leave the places they were born and travel to new places to start new careers.

Watt's rotative engine made a real difference in factories. Production increased as power became dependable. Other inventors focused on creating the high-pressure steam engine that Watt was afraid to use. Watt's engines were strong, but other inventors continued to increase the amount of steam used. By 1815, an American named Oliver Evans had created an engine that was fourteen times more powerful than Watt's. By the end of the century, steam engines seventy times more powerful were commonplace.

Oliver Evans was an American inventor who was born in Delaware in 1755 and died in 1819.

As the 1700s came to an end, many different inventors were working to create a steam-driven boat. In 1787, a man named James Rumsey built a boat that ran on steam. It went down the Potomac River at an average speed of 3 miles (5 km) per hour. Within two years, William Symington from Scotland created a 25-foot (8-m) long catamaran steamboat and a steam-powered side-wheel vessel called the *Charlotte Dundas* that reached a top speed of 7 miles (11 km) per hour. American Elijah Ormsbee did the same thing in 1792, as did Samuel Morey in 1793. These boats opened up the world to many, allowing them to move entire families, start new businesses, or ship their products and goods to places they couldn't reach before.

From Design to Practice

One of the primary people who made the steamboat work more efficiently was Robert Fulton. Born in Pennsylvania, Fulton was a painter who specialized in

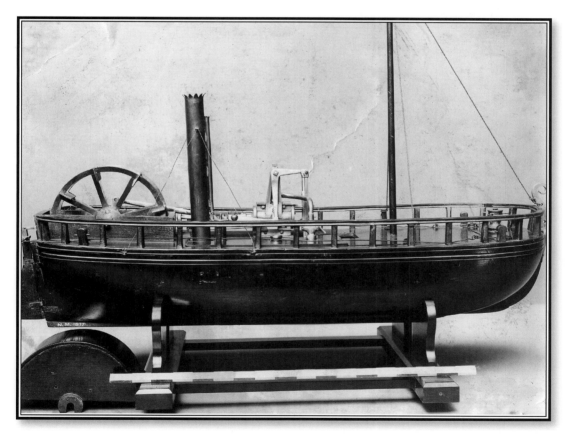

The Charlotte Dundas *was one of the first steamboats ever built.*

portraits, but he was eventually lured from blank canvases to steamships. In 1800, he invented the first submarine. He named it the *Nautilus* and tried to sell the design, but neither the English nor the French were interested. Nor were they interested in the underwater torpedoes he invented. When he tried to tell Napoléon about the steamboat he was working on, the French dictator was quoted as replying, "What, sir, would you make a ship sail against the wind and currents by lighting a bonfire under the deck? I pray you excuse me. I have to no time to listen to such nonsense."

Robert Fulton was an artist, engineer, and inventor. Born in Pennsylvania in 1765, his Clermont *was the first steamboat to become a commercial success.*

In 1807, Fulton designed a steamboat called the *Clermont.* Using Watt's engine, Fulton's boat was built by using the accumulated knowledge of others' work. It was also the first steamboat to become a commercial success.

Fulton's steamboat is usually referred to as the Clermont, *but its real name was the* North River Steamboat. *Fulton usually called it the* North River.

On August 7, 1807, Fulton put the *Clermont* into the Hudson River in New York. As the steam engine began to work, the deck shook, and smoke poured from the chimney. Those who witnessed the event were shocked to see a boat traveling against the current without any sails. Some thought that the "Devil had gone by on a raft." While at first the steamboat was thought of as an intriguing experiment, it was not long before it became one of the nation's most reliable forms of transportation. It was a boat that did not depend on the wind or the current. The *Clermont* traveled

The Clermont *traveled the Hudson River from New York City to Albany, New York, at a speed of 5 miles (8 km) per hour.*

all the way to Albany on her maiden voyage. The journey of 150 miles (241 km) took thirty-two hours at an average speed of 5 miles (8 km) per hour.

The next month, Fulton's steamship carried its first paying passengers. In 1808, he rebuilt his steamship and made some improvements to it. This model was bigger and stronger, and that summer, it was booked solid, with no room for any more passengers. Fulton was making a profit. Speculating that the western part of the United States needed reliable water transportation, too, Fulton hired Nicholas Roosevelt to construct another ship, called the *New Orleans,* which set sail from Pittsburgh, Pennsylvania, in September 1811 and arrived in New Orleans, Louisiana, in January 1812.

In 1813, Congress authorized steamships to carry mail, which helped people communicate more quickly. In 1819, the *Savannah* crossed the Atlantic, and one year later the steamship *James Watt* was launched. It had two Boulton and Watt engines in it, each one driving a paddle wheel. Two years later, the *Aaron Manby* was the first iron ship to be propelled by steam.

By 1825, steamboats were popping up all over the

The Great Western Steamship *traveled from Bristol, England, to New York City. The trip took twelve days and eighteen hours.*

waterways. They were used to transport people as well as cargo. Within a few years, steamboats were making regular transatlantic voyages, giving merchants new opportunities to trade their wares in faraway places.

Isambard Kingdom Brunel designed a steamship to cross the Atlantic Ocean regularly. Called the *Great Western,* it was launched in 1837 and made its first trip across the Atlantic in 1845. A few years later, Brunel also built the *Great Eastern,* which combined paddle wheels with a propeller. It was used to lay the transatlantic telegraph cable.

English engineer and inventor Richard Trevithick was born in 1771 and died in 1833.

On Another Front

At the same time some inventors were at work on the steamboat, others were focused on creating a high-pressure steam engine that could be used to propel a carriage. The man who built one of the first of these machines was Richard Trevithick.

As a child, Trevithick spent time wandering around in the mines where

Trevithick demonstrated the Catch-Me-Who-Can, *his third locomotive, on a circular track in London.*

his father worked. By the time he was nineteen, he was a consulting engineer. In 1801, he built his first steam locomotive. On Christmas Eve in London, his steam carriage carried its first passengers. Unlike modern locomotives,

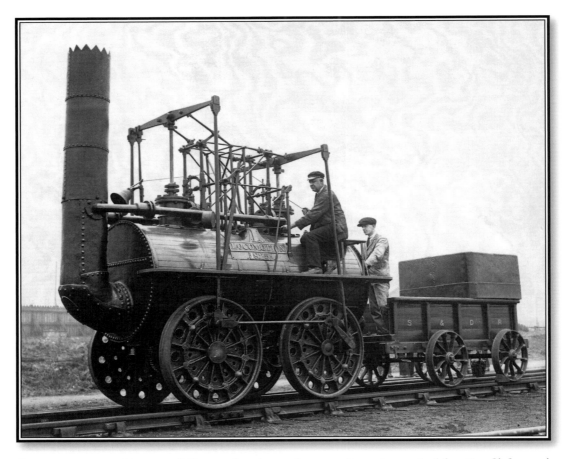

Two men operate one of the early steam locomotives invented by English engineer George Stephenson.

this machine was built to run on roads like an automobile, rather than on tracks like a train. Its primary purpose was to haul coal and ore out of the mines. In 1804, Trevithick's locomotive ran on a railway line and pulled 10 tons (9 t) of iron as well as seventy men. Unfortunately, the rails that were built to handle these machines were not up to the job. It would be several years before rails capable of reliably bearing the weight of locomotives came along.

Trevithick was an amazing inventor but a dismal businessman. He didn't have any idea how to market his inventions, and by the time he died, he was penniless.

The Father of the Railways

The man who would come to be known in England as the "father of the railways" was George Stephenson. From an early age he had been fascinated with machines, and when he got a job as an engineman at a coal mine, he had the opportunity to take apart Newcomen and Watt engines. He learned exactly how they worked, and soon his knowledge of engines earned him a promotion.

George Stephenson wanted to be the first person to build a locomotive.

In 1813, Stephenson discovered that a number of men were trying to build the first locomotive. He was determined to be the first to succeed because he believed that trains were the hallmark of the future. He was right.

A Prediction of the Future

According to biographer John Dixon, Stephenson once told a friend, "railways will supersede almost all other methods of conveyance in this country—when mail-coaches will go by railway, and railroads will become the great highway for the king and all his subjects. I know there are great and almost insurmountable difficulties to be encountered; but what I have said will come to pass as sure as you live."

In 1814, Stephenson built a locomotive that could carry 30 tons (27 t) up a hill at 4 miles (6 km) per hour. He called his locomotive the Blutcher. At almost the same time, a man named Colonel John Stevens was creating some of the same technology in the United States. He was granted the first railroad charter in North America in 1815. A decade later, he built a circular railway on which a steam locomotive ran at 12 miles (19 km) per hour. A few years earlier Stevens had also created a steamboat, the *Phoenix*, which worked as well as Fulton's *Clermont.*

Both steamboats and locomotives changed the world in countless ways. They made trade easier, travel swifter, and exploration simpler. The steam engine's role was vital in the development of these machines, but its usefulness did not stop there.

CHAPTER SIX

Taking Steam into the Future

The invention of the steam engine marked a new era in history. For the first time, people did not have to depend on unreliable water, wind, or animal power. As the world's demand for power grew, the steam engine was there to help meet those demands. That demand for power still exists today, and although other inventions have come along to replace steam power, it has not completely disappeared. Today, the technology can be seen in machines with *internal combustion* engines, such as cars, motorcycles, lawnmowers, and power saws.

New Developments

As the centuries passed, steam locomotives and steamships were continually improved. The technology,

After the steam engine was perfected, it was used for many different purposes. This horse-drawn fire engine relied on a steam-powered water pump.

however, was used for other purposes as well. In 1823, Jacob Perkins experimented with superheated steam in an invention he called a flash boiler. In the early 1840s, American inventor Paul Hodge created the first steam-powered fire engine. Other firefighters laughed at him. In 1853, Alexander Bonner Latta invented another fire engine that ran on steam. It was tested in Cincinnati, Ohio, and the city became the first to replace volunteers with a horse-drawn fire engine. In 1849, the first patent was issued for a percussion rock drill driven by steam power. In 1855, Joshua Stoddard patented the first steam *calliope,* a musical instrument that has steam whistles and is played with a keyboard. Two years later, the Otis brothers built the first steam-powered elevator in a five-story department store. They continued to build them for many years. They even had two of their steam-driven, hydraulic elevators installed in the Eiffel Tower in Paris, France.

The steam engine itself underwent a number of improvements. In 1854, John Elder developed the compound steam engine that included an additional cylinder. This allowed more power to be created with less fuel. Fifteen years later, Alexander Kirk upgraded the design to a triple expansion engine. This meant that what the original steam engine could do with 3 tons (2.7 t) of coal could now be done with 1 ton (0.9 t). In 1881, further advances were made when Werner von Siemens connected a steam engine to a *dynamo,* or a generator for producing electric power. That same year, Thomas Edison displayed a 300-horsepower dynamo at the Paris Exhibition. In the late 1800s, the steam turbine was developed, which was used in some huge steamships, such as the *Titanic,* and largely replaced reciprocating steam engines when it was perfected.

New Horizons for Railroads

Although steam engines continued to be developed for railroads, new inventions were coming along that would eventually make them obsolete. In 1892, Rudolf Diesel created his diesel engine, which slowly replaced steam engines on the railways. Diesel engines are more efficient and more

Rudolf Diesel was born in Paris, France, in 1858. On September 28, 1913, he was aboard the steamship Dresden *when he disappeared from the deck and was assumed to have drowned.*

powerful than steam engines. Because steam engines have boilers that can be as dangerous as bombs if broken, they must be regularly inspected for cracks. Diesel engines, on the other hand, are safer. The steam locomotive slowly lost its importance. By the end of the 1950s, the era of the steam locomotive was over. Steam is still important, but today steam turbines do the work instead of steam engines. Nuclear submarines are driven by turbines that receive their steam from boilers heated by nuclear reactors.

Steam still plays a part in modern life. In some parts of the world, such as China, Chile, and parts of the former Soviet Union, steam locomotives are still used. In fact, China has one of the biggest collections of working steam locomotives on the planet. It once operated thousands of them, carrying passengers daily from one place to another.

The Future of Power

Nuclear submarines use steam turbines. Steam is produced in a boiler that is heated by *atomic energy,* or energy that is produced by splitting atoms. Today, the nuclear energy used in power plants all over the world could not be adequately harnessed if the steam engine had not been created almost two hundred years ago. Nuclear power plants boil water to make steam to drive turbines. There are currently 103 such power plants in 31 states in the United States. They produce about 20 percent of the nation's electricity. The electricity production from nuclear power plants in the United States is more than that from power plants fueled by oil, natural gas, and hydropower. Only coal-fueled plants produce more power.

Steam engines may well play a role in the future if *fusion power* is ever developed. Fusion releases the energy that allows the sun to shine and powers the stars. It may be strong, but it is challenging to capture and control.

From the United Kingdom

"There are still very many difficulties but perhaps in a few decades we could have commercial fusion reactors in cities providing cheap, pollution-free power."

—Dr. Alan Sykes, United Kingdom Atomic Energy Authority

If developed, fusion power will provide limitless energy that is inexpensive and pollution-free. Just as in today's nuclear power plants, the steam turbine would be right there to help harness that energy and channel it to the right places.

The steam engine was a remarkable invention for several reasons. It came about through experimentation and the sharing of ideas over a long period of time. It developed slowly and became far more powerful than its inventors ever dreamed it would. It lifted the burden of labor from the backs of animals and people. Changing our way of life, it brought about a new era called the Industrial Age. It led to exploration, discovery, and growth for the world. The steam engine provided the basic technology for similar creations that continue to be used today and have enormous potential for the future.

Today, steam generators are used in nuclear power plants.

The Steam Engine: A Timeline

Hero of Alexandria creates a toy steam engine he calls an aeolipile.
p. 18

Thomas Savery patents the first crude steam engine.
p. 21

James Watt patents the first practical steam engine.
p. 32

A.D. 62 — **1654** — **1698** — **1712** — **1769** — **1781**

Otto von Guericke invents an air pump.
p. 17

Thomas Newcomen builds the first steam engine on top of a water-filled mine shaft and uses it to pump the water out.
p. 29

James Watt produces the first rotary-motion steam engine.
p. 34

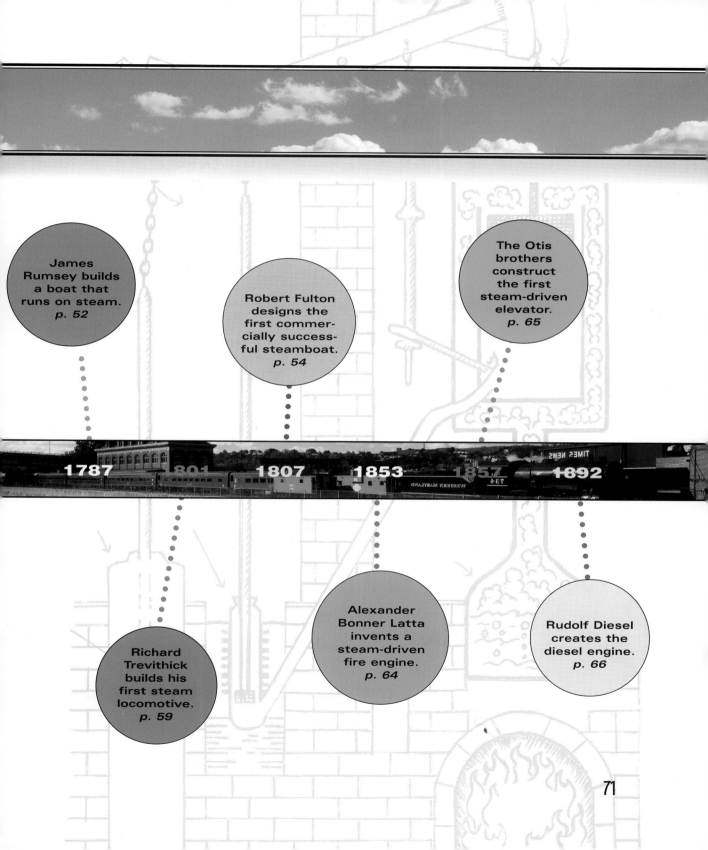

James Rumsey builds a boat that runs on steam.
p. 52

Robert Fulton designs the first commercially successful steamboat.
p. 54

The Otis brothers construct the first steam-driven elevator.
p. 65

1787   1801   1807   1853   1857   1892

Richard Trevithick builds his first steam locomotive.
p. 59

Alexander Bonner Latta invents a steam-driven fire engine.
p. 64

Rudolf Diesel creates the diesel engine.
p. 66

71

Glossary

air pressure: pressure exerted by the atmosphere

atmospheric pressure: pressure created by the weight of the atmosphere

atomic energy: energy released by a nuclear reaction, especially by fission or fusion

barrel organ: a mechanical instrument on which a tune is played by the action of a revolving cylinder fitted with pegs or pins that open pipe valves supplied by a bellows

boring machine: a machine that made it possible to drill perfectly round holes

calliope: a musical organ that is made of whistles powered by air or steam

compass: a tool that determines geographic direction through a needle aligned with the earth's magnetic field

cylinder: the chamber of a pump from which fluid is expelled by a piston

double-acting engine: a machine that can supply power in two directions

dynamo: electric generator

fusion power: nuclear reaction during which energy is released when nuclei combine to form more massive nuclei

hydraulics: of, involving, moved by, or operated by a fluid, especially water, under pressure

internal combustion: the combustion of fuel inside a cylinder

odometer: an instrument that indicates distance traveled by a vehicle

parallel motion: a jointed system of links, rods, or bars by which the motion of a reciprocating piece, such as a piston rod, may be guided, either approximately or exactly, in a straight line

patent: to receive a grant given by a government that confers upon the creator of an invention the sole right to make, use, and sell that invention for a set period of time

pneumatics: the study of the mechanical properties of air and other gases

quadrant: an early instrument for measuring the altitude of celestial bodies

smokeless furnace: a furnace that could burn fuel without emitting any smoke

tangentially: in a way that is moving or making contact at a single point or along a line; in a way that is touching but not intersecting

vacuum: volume in which the pressure is significantly lower than atmospheric pressure

To Find Out More

Books

Gardner, Esther. *Steam Locomotive: A Story of the Golden Age of Steam in the United States.* Overland Park, KS: Leathers Publishing, 1999.

Kras, Sara Louise. *The Steam Engine.* Broomall, PA: Chelsea House Publishers, 2003.

Siegel, Beatrice. *The Steam Engine.* New York: Walker and Company, 1986.

Sproule, Anna. *James Watt: Master of the Steam Engine.* Woodbridge, CT: Blackbirch Press, 2001.

Zimmermann, Karl. *Steam Locomotives: Whistling, Chugging, Smoking Iron Horses of the Past.* Honesdale, PA: Boyds Mills Press, 2004.

Web Sites

The History of Steam Engines

http://inventors.about.com/library/inventors/
blsteamengine.htm

About.com's site on the history of steam engines.

How Steam Engines Work

http://travel.howstuffworks.com/steam.htm

An inside, animated look at how steam engines work.

The Steam Engine

http://www.egr.msu.edu/~lira/supp/steam

Textbook summary of the development of steam engines with interactive links

Organizations

The New England Wireless and Steam Museum, Inc.

1300 Frenchtown Road
East Greenwich, RI 02818-1424
(401) 885-0545

Steam Engine Museum

PO Box 56
Mabel, MN 55954
(507) 493-5350

Index

About the Author

Tamra Orr is a full-time writer from Portland, Oregon. She has a degree in secondary education from Ball State University. She has written more than forty nonfiction books, including *Indonesia, Turkey,* and *Slovenia* in the Enchantment of the World series for Children's Press and *School Violence: Halls of Hope, Halls of Fear* for Franklin Watts. She is the homeschooling mother of four, ranging in age from eight to twenty, and life partner to Joseph.

To write this book, Orr spent hours on the Internet, in the library, and with her father learning about thermodynamics. She went to her state museum to see engine displays—and wishes she had taken shop in school instead of home economics.